True Ghost Stories

Dr. Kenzo Amariyo PhD.(A.M.)

True Ghost Stories
Working with the Other Side

The events in this little book of stories are true events. Each one was an experience the author had. Her encounters with the spirit world has spanned all her life starting at 5 years old.

The stories are not embellished they are what they are. Most of the occurrences are in order to facilitate healing, but not all.

The purpose of this book is to continue to shed some light on the other realms of life in hope to assist those who do not believe too believe.

The events mirror the authors belief that there is life past death and that death and birth are simply different sides of the same coin.

Her encounters confirm for her that:

> *"...there is no death – only a change of worlds..."*

Chief Seattle

Contents

Thank You for Purchasing this Book

Other Titles by the Author

The Effects of Shamanic Healing and Other Healing Practices on General Well-Being – Independently Published 2018 by Amazon

Poems for Loved Ones – Independently Published 2018 by Amazon

Urinalysis, Alkalinity and Well-Being – Independently Published 2018 by Amazon

True Ghost Stories

A Cleansing

It was early evening, I had just heard about a suicide in a trailer park nearby. A youngish man who had become depressed had not been seen for four days. He lived alone other than with his beloved cats. He had put a pistol to his head and pulled the trigger. No-one had realized he was dead, or at-least not until they decided to check his trailer.

I don't want to even imagine how horrendous the scene must have looked, not to mention the smell as it was summer in Arizona. The trailer had been closed up for a few days and I don't even want to think about the trauma the cats must have gone through, such a waste of life.

Sadness was all around and this particular evening, I felt very strongly that I needed to go and spiritually cleanse the trailer park. When someone takes their own life, it is said to open up a gateway for negative spirits to enter the space. I needed to cleanse the area and remove all negative spirits, thus closing the gate again.

I approached his trailer and saw the spirit of the man sitting next to the trailer on a log, he looked at me with regret and said *'I didn't mean to do it' 'I didn't mean to pull the trigger so hard'.* There was not a lot I could say to him, I told him he needed to follow the light and with that, he was gone.

I burnt some herbs and cleansed around the trailer leaving some burning herbs on a tree stump close by, I continued to walk around the park praying and cleansing the area from all unwanted energies.

It wasn't until I reached the creek at the other side of the park that I could feel a really negative spirit. I had been standing facing the creek listening to the song of the water as I often did, when I felt the presence of the spirit behind me. I could feel that the spirit wanted to push me over the edge, into the creek to harm me. I turned around to face him and told him to follow the light, he was reluctant, but with that he was gone.

This is why suicide is not a good way out, it creates so much negativity for those left behind and in the vicinity.

I continued on until I felt the park cleansing was complete and that the park was free of negative spirits. Then I went on my way.

Bad Energy

It was a dark winter night, it had been a long day and I was drying my hair in front of the bedroom window as I would normally do, when suddenly I could feel that a man had suddenly entered the bedroom, a spirit, and not a nice spirit.

I continued on with drying my hair to see or feel what he was going to do. Suddenly I could feel that he had a piece of wire (not physically) wrapped around both hands leaving a couple of feet between them, I could feel that he wanted to throw it around my neck and pull it tight. I quickly spun around to face him, he was a very mean man and the vehemence he held towards women was very strong. I ordered him to leave, he was gone in seconds.

On reflection I felt he was connected to the neighbour's house. I cleansed our house and placed a protection around it, something I had not yet done as we had only just moved in.

From that evening, I was aware that he stood outside the neighbour's house at night looking up through our window with that same vehemence. The energy from him was so strong, even I felt like moving away from the window, away from his stare. It felt as if he was aiming something at me and that if I stayed there it would come straight through the window. He had to go.

The energy this man or spirit gave off was so strong that even the dog would not go all the way up the road at night, he would just stop and look ahead as if he was looking at something or someone.

It was time to remove him, time to send him to the light. I collected the things that I felt I needed to cleanse the area and in the evening, which is the only time he came around I set out in prayer and with protection.

As soon as I had walked a few steps towards the neighbour's house he was there, right in front of me, challenging me. I knew I needed to stay strong and centred as I knew I could not trust him. He looked me straight in the eye and said *"You can't make me go"* and with that, I told him to follow the light, he wasn't welcome there anymore. He hesitated, but he knew I meant it, I told him again and with that he was gone. I cleansed the whole area whilst praying over it using salt where necessary for protection.

He knew he would have to go, I felt he had been there for years and he was probably the reason why the neighbour's house had never sold.

After the clearing, the dog was happy to go up and down the road, he came with me when I went to perform the clearing. It was as if he knew that I was going to remove the spirit. After that, there was no bad energy around the house, and I was able to go back to standing in front of the window at night.

Find My Son

It was a usual cruise, going between Sydney Harbour and the South Pacific Islands, I had had my usual day massaging. In the evenings it was nice to be on deck or hang out with friends, this evening, I felt I wanted to stay in my cabin, to connect with spirit.

It was getting late, I needed to be up early the next day, so I put down my pen which was always busy writing in my diary and went to sleep.

I never locked my cabin door as there were a couple of crew members that I used to do healing with, so they knew that my door was always open.

I was fast asleep when I started to sense a presence of someone, a man in my room, it was a heavy presence and strong enough to awake me from a deep sleep. I looked around and realized no-one was there. I went back to sleep and the same feeling awoke me again. Feeling a bit uneasy with such a strong presence, I locked my door and went back to sleep.

Then it happened, this time the presence was so strong I sat bolt upright and remembering that the door was locked, I realized I was in the presence of a spirit. I grabbed my pen and paper as I knew that I was about to receive a message.

The spirit was of a tall man, in his 40's, he had worked on ships and died suddenly and unexpectedly of a heart attack leaving behind his wife and children.

I asked him what he wanted, he said *'find my son, he is on this ship, tell him to let me go, he is keeping me earth-bound, tell him I love him.'*

With that the spirit was gone. I was left wondering how on earth I was supposed to find his son, I didn't know whether that was a crew member or a passenger. That is all I was left with.

The next morning the message weighed heavily on my mind, I prayed to Spirit, asking for help in finding this man.

We were at the end of the cruise, it was the evening before passengers disembarked and I was aware that if I didn't find him tonight, and he was a passenger, then it would be too late.

I spent some time wandering around the ship walking in passenger areas, walking around the decks in hope that if he was a passenger, I would be drawn to him or him to me, but nothing happened.

It was getting late so I decided to call it a day and go to my cabin to write in my diary as I quite often did, with the door wide open so people felt they could drop in. I finished my entry and got up to close the door just as one of the firemen went by.

He always used to say *hi* but this time he stopped, so I made conversation with him asking him where he was from and whether he had brothers and sisters. Slowly but surely I started to feel that he was the son.

I asked him about his dad and if his dad used to work on ships, he said *'yes'* and I said, *'he died of a heart attack didn't he?'* He looked so shocked, once again, I had been led to the right person.

I invited him in and explained to him that I had a message from his dad. He said he was a devoted Catholic and found it hard to believe that I had a message from a dead person.

I went on to describe what his dad had said to me, and told him the message, his eyes welled up as he went on to tell me and show me that he wore his dad's ring on a chain around his neck, and how much he missed his dad.

He said he was only 11years old at the time and it broke his heart when his dad died. He was now in his twenties, a young man with so much to offer and so full of grief.

He went on to ask me how to let his dad go, so we talked a little about how to release him.

It was now the early hours of the morning, the crew member still wasn't sure whether *letting dad go* was going to make a difference so he decided that he would try it in the morning and let me know how it went.

I was happy with that, at the end of the day, I had done as I had been asked; I had found the son and delivered the message.

The next day I saw the young man and he didn't need to tell me that he had followed my suggestions, I could see he had received a release, he was smiling, his eyes were sparkling and he had a lightness around him, around his spirit.

Nevertheless, he told me that he had done as I suggested and that he couldn't believe the difference it had made to him and how much lighter and happier he felt. He couldn't thank me enough and went on his way.

I saw him a few times after that, but that was the only time we had a real talk.

Forgive Yourself

I was in Sedona – Arizona. I had a man lying face down on my massage couch. He had been suffering with severe back pain for several years, he had seen doctors, surgeons, specialists, but no-one could find anything wrong with him. All that they knew was that it was getting worse and soon, he would be in a wheelchair.

I started the massage as I usually did with relaxing music playing in the background and working on the lower limbs. Knowing that he suffered great pain I took care to give him a deep but gentle massage. I worked on his back for quite a while and moved as I always did up towards his head to do some healing.

I placed my hands on his head, closed my eyes and allowed energy to flow through me. After a couple of minutes I opened my eyes and to the right of me, or the left of him, I could see a little girl, she looked about 2 years old, with blonde curly hair and a beautiful face.

It seemed a little odd at that moment so I continued on, just to be told by Spirit that I needed to ask him who this little girl was. I resisted as I thought he might think I was crazy!! But in the end, after being nagged to ask him I did.

I am so glad I followed Spirit. He went on to say that that was his little girl, he was a truck driver and was getting ready to leave for another journey. His wife and little girl were outside ready to say goodbye to him, but unbeknown to them both, whilst they were saying there goodbye's the little girl had gone around to the front of the truck and sat down in front of the wheel.

They did not realize this until it was too late, as the engine roared, the large wheels of the truck slowly edged forward and crushed her; she was dead.

It had been the worse time of his life, he had been carrying around so much grief, so much guilt feelings, blaming himself and feeling that he had killed his little girl. All these negative emotions, all this emotional pain was taking its toll on him, this guilt had been slowly creeping up his spine causing pain and was slowly crippling him. He really needed to forgive himself.

I talked to him about forgiveness and reassured him that it wasn't his fault, we looked at that perhaps we all have a designated time on this earth, and that something will remove us all one day.

I stayed with him awhile while he talked some more and we talked about his feelings. He was pretty taken back by the fact that I could see her and describe her but that was the evidence he needed to know that I was telling the truth. It was then that he knew he needed to forgive himself in order to be able to walk properly again, pain free.

He got up off the couch, and too his amazement, he actually said *"I know longer have any pain"*. He was quite surprised about this and began to move around and do the things that he knew he couldn't normally do. To his amazement, he could do them. He was healed, he had found the key to unlock the door to his healing process.

I continued to offer him advice on how to remain healed and he recognized that it was his grief and guilt that was crippling him.

He left a changed man that day, a healed man and that was the only time I ever saw him.

Let Me Go

It was a usual day in Port, most of the passengers had got off the ship to enjoy tours and the freedom to wander around so the salon was quiet. A beauty therapist had asked for some healing, she had been feeling quite down, her fiancé had died in an accident several years ago. She still wore the engagement ring, she had never had another boyfriend and was reluctant to move on in her life.

She lay down on the couch whilst I sat at the head, I lay my hands on her head and almost instantly her boyfriend not only appeared, but spoke. It was an unpleasant feeling, as I felt he was going to use my body or at least my voice and I could hear the strain in his voice as he uttered the words through me – *"Let me go….You are keeping me earth bound…..You are holding me back"*

The voice felt and sounded distorted which was quite freaky. As I spoke the words to her the tall barricade that she had built around her heart began to crumble, as it crumbled, it opened up the way for the reservoir of tears to come tumbling down. She was finally finding a release, finally she was able to *let go* and open up the way for herself to move on.

This wasn't the end of her healing, not by a long way, it was merely the beginning, she had a long way to go, but now she had released her fiancé, she had created a space for healing to commence.

Not only was this the beginning of her freedom but his too.

Little Spirit Girl

I was sitting at my desk in my cabin when I was aware that out of the corner of my eye I could see a little girl, I looked, but she was gone. I continued writing and became aware again that she was standing behind me but to the side. I slowly looked again, but again she was gone.

She looked a shy little girl with shoulder length hair and a nice face, I continued writing. Once again, she came back, but this time I didn't turn my head, I could just see her out of the corner of my eye.

I spoke to her, telling her that she doesn't need to be afraid and that I won't hurt her. She replied *"you can see me"*, *"yes"* I replied. It seemed to make her feel more relaxed so I turned towards her and this time she stayed.

We looked at each other for a few seconds and then I asked her what she was doing there. She replied, *"I am looking for my family, we were all on a ship and it sank"*. The feeling I had was that they were all dead so I told her *"you will not find your family here, you must follow the light otherwise you may become earth-bound"* She disappeared.

The next day I was busy doing my massage when she re-appeared, she stood there smiling at me. Now feeling very relaxed with me, she watched me working and then when I began to do some healing, she put her hands on the passenger I was healing and helped.

Her little hands looked so sweet, she must have only been about eight or nine. She closed her eyes and participated in the healing. I reminded her that she needed to follow the light and with that, she disappeared and I never saw her again.

Release

Mark was a young easy going man who had had many challenges in his life, challenges with his family, friends and his work life. Mark had a brother that he was especially close too, someone that he looked up too and admired a lot, despite his brother's self-created difficulties.

One day Mark was informed that his brother was dead, an accidental death so they say, this had a major impact on Mark as the only person he looked up too was now gone.

Time went on and Mark found himself thinking and feeling much the same as his brother had felt, very lonely, insignificant and as if the world could not accept him as he was. Such feelings were leading him deeper into depression and deeper into the habits that his brother had been caught up in causing a negative cycle of self-destruction.

When Mark came to me, he felt he had nowhere else to go, the medication hadn't really helped, the support with his habits was not really working and he felt that all was lost and the only way out was to join his brother.

As I started to work on Mark, I could feel that his brother was with us, he was there in the room. The connection between them was so strong; I asked his brother if there was anything that he wanted to say to Mark, and there was, so I relayed the message to Mark.

The message was about getting on with life and letting him go. I also asked Mark if there was anything he would like to say to his brother, there was; so Mark spent quite a few minutes talking to his brother, telling him how much he had looked up to him and how much he missed him.

They had quite an intimate time together but they both knew that it was time to say 'Good-Bye'.

When the time felt right, I guided Mark to say his farewells and explained to them both that there were spirit beings, helpers, waiting to take his brother to the light.

As I watched, a bright light appeared and the brother started to ascend with the beings, I could see that the brother was looking back at Mark but I wasn't sure why. Suddenly, Mark started to feel that there was a cord that was attached between him and his brother at the third Chakra (solar plexus area); and the higher his brother went the more Mark started to feel as if the cord was pulling him up off the couch.

They still hadn't let each other go, even though they had both said their goodbyes. I quickly cut the cord that was keeping the brothers connected and Mark suddenly felt as if his whole back had suddenly come back down onto the couch.

The connection was broken, Mark was now able to look and see his brother as he ascended with the spirit beings to the light.

Mark came for a couple more sessions after that, but his feelings of being lonely and insignificant had gone, he was once again starting to feel like his own self and starting to look forward to the rest of his life in the knowledge that his brother was safe.

He no longer felt that he wanted to die to be with his brother and consequently came off his medication and started to get on with the rest of his life.

Releasing Grief

It was a few weeks before I was due to go to my first ship, I was doing normal things around the house when I had a vision. It was of myself standing at the back of the ship with an older gentleman, he had gone on the cruise to scatter the ashes of his late wife. It was quite a strange experience as I had never been on a ship before, yet it all looked so real.

Several weeks into the cruise, I had completely forgotten about the vision, I was busy going about my usual day which was full of passengers wanting a massage. An older gentleman came for his half hour back massage, which wasn't unusual, a lot of older people came on the cruise.

As the music played softly in the background and the ship gently rolled back and forth, I poured a little oil which I had made up myself, into my hands and gently rubbed my hands together to warm the oil.

As I gently laid my hands upon his back I was suddenly struck with grief, I knew it wasn't my grief, it was his. With tears rolling down my cheeks (from his grief) I said to him *"What is all this grief?"* But before he had a chance to answer, I remembered the vision and said to him: "*I know why you are here, your wife has died and you are here to scatter her ashes".*

He swung his head around in disbelief, complete shock, *"how do you know that?"* he said; I replied *"I had a vision of you before I came to ship, I didn't know what you looked like, but I knew why you were going to be here".*

By this time, the man was completely in tears, sobbing on my shoulder, he used to come on cruises with his wife, but now she had died he wasn't going to come anymore. He wanted to come one last time, in memory of her and scatter her ashes at sea.

The turmoil leading up to him coming had made him leave the ashes at home, but what I felt to offer him was that at sunset, that day, we would meet at the back of the ship and we would offer a prayer and say farewell to her in order to assist him in letting her go. As he did not have her ashes, I felt to use a glass of water to symbolize the ashes and the letting go of that special person in his life, for her, a returning home.

We met just before sunset, it was a beautiful evening, the sky was still blue, the orange from the sun was painting a beautiful picture on the horizon and we spent a few quiet minutes before we commenced the goodbyes.

When the time seemed right, I said a few words for her and he said his goodbyes and with a few more words and a blessing, we poured the water over board to release not only her, but also all the grief.

It was a lovely way to let her go and for him to start the healing process.

There was a passenger entertainment night that night, and he had written a poem about his wife which he was going to read out on stage. He desperately wanted me to be there, but I didn't make it. It wasn't going to be until very late and I was completely drained from sharing some of his grief. Once in my cabin, and after releasing the remainder of grief that I was carrying for him, I sank into a very deep sleep of which I did not wake up until the next morning.

I saw him briefly the next morning as it was time for the passengers to disembark, I had gone to look for him to make sure he was ok. He was easy to find as he was tall and well dressed in country and western style clothes and boots, he even had the country and western style hat, all of which he wore with confidence and pride.

He had missed me being at the entertainment night but understood. I had a final chat with him and reminded him that he does have reasons to keep going. That was the last time I saw or heard from him until................

It was 2001, I was in Australia visiting and I had this feeling I needed to go and see, not necessarily a psychic but someone who was in touch with the other side, but I wanted someone who was following a North American Indian path.

An old friend knew who I needed to see. I bought some gifts to leave for her as an offering rather than money and as soon as she saw me she said: *"I have this older gentleman here, he just wants to say hello"* at first I didn't know who he was, but then she said: *"he's dressed in country and western clothes, he has a big hat, he's showing me his belt with horses on it".*

I left there with a big smile and a deep sense of peace. I didn't know what had happened to him, I didn't know if his time was up or whether he had ended his life, but what I did know was he was still filled with appreciation for what I had done for him.

That blessed me no-end.

Removing the Stake

It was late in the afternoon, Maria had come to see me because life had become too overwhelming. Her constant tiredness and weariness coupled with the hurts of the past and present were all taking their toll on her.

I spent some time assessing Maria's needs, or at least trying too, there was so much going on for her and in her, she was all over the place, flitting from one thing to another, it was hard to keep up with her.

After about 20 minutes, I asked her to lay on the couch, I could feel her apprehension, but I could also feel her hope that this session would bring some release to what was becoming a never ending life of pain.

I performed my usual ceremony and asked Spirit to be with us, I followed my usual routine and tracked along her body and once I was sure which Chakras were compromised I commenced the cleansing.

As Maria started to relax, the pressures of life started to fall away, the relief which this was bringing also made a way for her to release some of the hurts of the past and present.

Tears slowly began to fall down her cheeks as quiet sobs came from the depth of her heart, she was finally finding some release, release from all the hurts, the let downs, the disappointments, relief from the accusations and abandonment. So much pain and heartache in such a small body. Where she had gained the strength from to keep going only she knows, many would already have given up, but not Maria, she had an inner strength that kept her hanging in there, she had someone and something to keep going for.

The healing had been going on for nearly an hour now, I had cleansed all that I had seen, but yet, I felt very strongly that there was a crystallization somewhere that I had not found.

I asked Spirit for help, to be shown where the issue lay, but I was told that she needed to find it herself as part of her healing.

Crystallization of negative energy can happen when the negative energy has been in the Luminous Energy Field for a long time. The energy can take a form, but the form is only metaphorically speaking it is not literal.

I asked Maria how she was feeling and she said while sobbing, that she felt she had a stake sticking in her, this was the information I was looking for.

I asked her to show me where the stake was, I followed her hands to her diaphragm area, I carefully felt around the crystallization and took hold of what she felt to be a stake. After loosening it off, I pulled it from her, you could see the relief on her face. I continued to work on the area bringing healing, until what had felt like a hole, closed up and was just feeling like a bruise.

I completed the remainder of the healing and allowed Maria time to process what had happened, it was a huge healing that she had been through and the look of relief on her face was noticeable.

Something that had been affecting her for a very long time had gone, it was now lifted and she knew it.

For the first time in a long time, Maria felt she was taller, the load had been so heavy she had felt quite short, now she was able to hold her head up high and walk tall.

Maria left a different person that day, a much lighter person. She came back for several more sessions after that and went from strength to strength.

Sarah's Healing

It was 4:20pm my time, I had just scheduled a healing session for mid-week, but the healing wasn't going to wait that long: I felt to start the session now.

I journeyed to a place far away and entered into the Tipi with Sarah, the log fire was burning and the sweet pungent smell of sweet grass was filling the air, she lay on her back on the couch that had been prepared for her. She looked quite relaxed and as she lay back, and closed her eyes, her soft fair hair fell back off her face. The healing had commenced.

As I stood beside her at her left side I could see that there were many *red areas or lumps* running down from her left inner arm down her side and towards her hip. I lifted up the scalpel under the direction of my spirit physician and I began to cut away the red areas. As I began to cut I realized they were all interconnected. It was like cutting away seaweed, lumps all joined together by interconnecting fibres. As I cut the red areas out, the connecting network easily pulled away from her body. This network went all the way down to her hip and into her groin.

After removing all the red areas, it was now looking like a very open and raw wound. I was guided to another nodule or red area, just under the upper body which I had missed, hidden from view because of her lying on her back. After carefully removing it, I was given a jug of what looked like water to pour over the open wounds.

As the water or liquid touched the open wounds, it was like cold water hitting something hot, it was like steam coming up from the wounds, but without any sound. As the steam or mist settled, I could see that it had sealed all the open wounds, it had formed a transparent skin type covering, offering protection.

Following this, I placed a clear quartz crystal upon her third eye whilst I placed my hands on her left wrist. Energy was channelled upwards towards her body, I then placed my left hand on her groin, pointing up towards the body; energy was now travelling in both directions through my hands and into Sarah. As the energy met in the middle, it looked like fork lightening as both streams of energy clashed, revitalizing the areas bringing healing.

Sarah was now beginning to sweat, the log fire was burning brightly, and the now potent smell of burning sage was filling the air. I smudged her entire body with the burning sage, using a feather to fan the healing smoke around her.

Sarah continued to perspire, her body now starting to gently shake; she was going through a massive healing. It wasn't long before she began to vomit, at first she was bringing up a large black mass which seemed difficult for her to get out so I pulled the rest of it out. This was followed by a thick green substance, I gave her sips of fluids, this enabled her body to continue to purge, she vomited again and again, this time it was a lot clearer and frothy, I continued to offer her sips of fluid until all vomiting had subsided.

She lay there sweating, gently shaking, I wrapped her up in skins to keep her warm and enable her body to sweat out all that it did not want, by this time she was falling asleep, into a deep sleep. I placed an amethyst in her left hand, a rose quartz in her right hand, I left the clear quartz on her forehead and placed obsidian at her feet.

The fire was topped up and the sage continued to burn as Sarah went through the remainder of her healing. I sat crossed legged on a skin beside her, gently rocking backwards and forwards as I quietly chanted a song.

The air was thick and heavy, yet filled with peace and a sense of a miracle, Sarah quietly slept.

Some hours later..........

Much time had passed, it was now dark outside and peace filled the air, Sarah had stopped perspiring, but her hair was drenched with perspiration that was now beginning to dry from the heat of the log fire.

Slowly she started to come back from where ever she had been, I sensed that where ever her journey had taken her, it was to re-claim lost parts of her soul. As she became more alert, I helped her to sit up a little, as she was still quite weak. She managed to slowly have a few mouthfuls of broth which would help to give her some strength back.

Silence filled the Tipi, there was no need to speak, what was done was done, there was no point trying to explain it away with words that fall short of all miracles. It isn't what you can explain that is always important, but what you experience, especially when the experience is beyond our language and understanding.

Time passed, it was time for Sarah to leave, I helped her off the couch and out into the bright night, where the darkness of the sky had fallen over the landscape, the stars shone in all their glory and the whisper of the wind could be heard rustling through the trees.

It was done, she had received her healing; she had re-claimed the lost parts of her soul.

I sat a while longer and bathed in the warmth of the fire and the serenity that filled the Tipi.................when the time was right, and when instructed to do so by Spirit, I returned, I journeyed back.

Soul Retrieval & Post Traumatic Stress

Lilly was a lovely young girl, very bright and reflected a happy balanced girl getting ready to enter into her teens. Yet despite what showed on the outside, within was a very different story.

Lilly had been involved in a tragic accident several years earlier and although she had received much psychological support to help her come to terms with it and work through it, it had still left an imprint in her Luminous Energy Field. She was still traumatised.

Quite often, when tragic or traumatic events occur in our lives, a part of us can flee. It is these very parts that need to be recovered or retrieved, healed and re-integrated into the person.

Post-Traumatic Stress was still very evident in Lilly, the anxiety, the tears, the original wounding so easily showed itself. It was time for Lilly to find the lost part of herself.

As Lilly was so young, and under the direction of my spirit helper, I decided to use a Galvanic Skin Response (GSR) monitor, the monitor measures activity via sending out minute electrical impulses into your fingers (which are not detectable to the individual). These electrical impulses react with the minute changes in perspiration related to stress and anxiety. By using the GSR monitor, I was able to measure and direct the healing in relation to Lilly's anxiety levels to affect a more comprehensive healing.

As Lilly was so young, I was aware that she would have limited experience at defining how she was feeling or what she was experiencing on a Spiritual level, so through using the GSR monitor, I was able to perform a healing session that was not only successful, but also required less participation from Lilly.

I guided and accompanied Lilly on her deep descent into the lower world where she needed to go in order to find the lost part of herself. Although her descent into the lower world was relatively easy, it took quite a while before Lilly was ready to actually *meet* that part of her as it also meant she would *re-live* momentarily, what that part was feeling at the time, including fear, anxiety and the trauma.

We spent much time preparing Lilly for this *meeting* and we waited until her anxiety levels had reached a certain low, which was then reflected on the GSR monitor. Spirit had already instructed me as to what level would be safe and productive in introducing her to her lost part.

Had I introduced her too early, she was at risk of re-living all the trauma without receiving the healing. NOT what we wanted! With guidance, Lilly eventually met her lost part, the part of her spirit that had left during the accident. I stood beside her all the way to ensure she was safe and she spent quite a while assisting that part of her spirit to heal. This was done through love and compassion, through forgiveness and building a bond, a relationship with that part.

That frightened little girl needed to feel loved and safe in order to agree to return with her, if she didn't, she may not have come back with her and could have split off or broken away again at any time.

As it was, she did feel safe and loved and although very apprehensive, we were able to get that part back safe and sound and re-introduce it into Lilly. Re-introducing a missing part of someone's spirit isn't always easy, but it must become a very integral part of, in this case Lilly, in order for it to stay which was why Lilly was going to need to look after and nurture that little girl, that little spirit in order for them both to completely heal and become a fully integrated part of Lilly once again.

The Silent Witness

Tanya was a middle-aged woman in a long term relationship. She was very much into spiritual things and clearly understood about energy and the spiritual side of life. She came to me for some healing after a significant event. The healing session it-self was not anything exceptional, but the event she experienced is worth sharing. Here I will share her story, these are my words of her verbal account.

It was New Year's Eve 2010, Tanya and her partner, a good hearted man, had decided to stay home to see the New Year in. They decided to watch the firework display on the T.V. at midnight. They were quietly chatting to each other and had drank only a couple of glasses of Champagne, so neither of them were intoxicated.

During the conversation, Tanya noticed a distinct change in the atmosphere, she felt there was suddenly a very hostile environment around her partner. She asked him what was wrong, but was met with a hostile response of *"oh nothing"*.

Quite disturbed about the sudden change and completely oblivious to anything wrong that she may have said, she responded with *"now what have I said wrong"* which was met with more hostility. Tanya went on to respond with *"all I wanted was a quiet drink to see the New Year in"* which resulted in her partner saying *"you wanted a drink, you can have a drink, here"*, and with that, he stood up and too her amazement, he proceeded to pour what would have been over half a bottle of Champagne over her head.

She sat still, frozen to her seat and for a brief moment she felt a deep concern for her safety. As she wiped the Champagne out of her eyes, she was in time to see him raise his hand to hit her across the head with the empty Champagne bottle. At that same moment, (and all this happened in seconds), she recollects seeing and sensing a presence, a spirit, an energy, somewhat like a cloak or perhaps an orb come straight through the wall behind her, covering her completely, like a blanket; and with that, a sense of calm came over her; she knew she would be alright no matter what happened. She sensed the same energy not only cover her, but extend itself right up to her partner, to at least his hand with the bottle in it. At that moment her partner seemed to come to his senses and put the bottle down.

Tanya, in absolute disbelief, left the room to clean herself up. Needless to say, she remained apart from him for a while before going to bed.

Even now, when I see her, she still can't believe the amazing way that Spirit protected her, the sheer fact that the protection was there instantaneously was such a blessing. She didn't have to call on it, nor *conjure* it up, it just was.

If nothing else, this serves to remind us that when we serve Spirit, we are protected and help is there when we need it.

In the Dark of the Night

I was only 5 years old at the time. I lived in a cottage, sharing a bedroom with my sister, she was one year older. It was a nice bedroom, overlooking the fields. But at night, it took on a different shade, a shade of grey.

It happened for many consecutive nights, I would climb into bed and as I stared at the small pink printed flowers on the wallpaper, he would appear. He came through the wall that adjoined our room to my parent's room. He was tall, wore dark clothes and a big black jacket. He was quite scary.

My sister was always asleep, she never did see him, and up until this day, no-one knew he existed. He used to come through the wall, across the bedroom passing my sisters bed, heading straight for me. I would lie there, heart pounding as I peeped over the blankets to watch him walk by and disappear into the big dark wardrobe that stood across from the foot of my bed.

Every morning I would get up and check inside the wardrobe to make sure he wasn't still in it. This had gone on for quite some time, but then, this one particular night, I decided I wasn't afraid of him and wasn't going to hide away under the blankets. I was going to keep my face in full view and watch him.

This particular night he came as normal from what seemed like through the flowers on the wall, he walked across the room as normal but he must have known I was looking at him because he suddenly swung his head around and looked right at me. My heart nearly came out of my chest and I quickly hid my face under the covers; but then I changed my mind as I wanted to see him go.

I bravely uncovered my face to find him still standing there, even his hair was very dark; he was so scary. He then beckoned me to go to him, he wanted me to go with him. I didn't go because I didn't know if I should and I couldn't work out how I could go with him when I knew he wasn't real, real that is like I was, I knew he was in a different form; I somehow knew he was a ghost.

That night, he didn't go into the wardrobe as he had all the other times, he went out of the window. Had I followed him as he wanted me too, I would have also gone out of the upstairs window. I don't know whether he really did want to harm me or whether he just wanted me to follow him, but either way, had I gone with him I probably wouldn't have been here today to tell the story. I never saw him again after that.

I Knew Who He Was

It was early evening, I was making my way home from a friend's house. I wasn't very old, I would have been around eight or nine. On my way home I came across a bully, a mean nasty boy who decided it would be fun to throw me down a dis-used grain store.

The wire fencing was old and broken from people pulling at it constantly and from lack of maintenance. As I glanced down the concrete grain store I was well aware how deep it was, how far down he was planning on throwing me.

Fear started to take hold as he and his four friends grabbed me, they were so intent on throwing me down there with no concern as to whether I would live or die.

I grabbed onto the old wire fence and held on as tight as I could whilst four horrid boys tried with all their might to pull me off it. I was squeezing so hard I could feel my own finger nails digging into the palms of my hands. With them hitting and punching my hands, I didn't know how long I could hold on and no-one was around.

Whilst they were trying to pry my fingers off the wire fence, I naturally looked up to the skies and called on God / Spirit for help. To my amazement, I felt someone come right up behind me, I felt him press his body against mine as he placed his hands over my hands. I knew who He was.

With this extraordinary miracle, I realized that I know longer needed to hold on so tight because I could feel His hands holding my hands on the wire fence whilst these monsters were still slapping and prying my hands. I can still remember today hearing one of them saying: *"Why is she so strong? How come we can't get her hands off it? There are four of us and only one of her".* With that, I began to loosen my grip as I knew I was safe in His hands.

At that time, the ring leaders' father appeared and sent the boys home whilst promising his own son a hiding when he got home.

I went home shaken but knowing I was in the safe hands of the Lord.

His Warmth

It was a lovely hot day in Australia, I had felt to go camping this particular night, I would be staying alone on 100 acres which belonged to a therapist I was friends with. I hadn't checked the weather as it didn't seem to matter as I felt deep within that I needed to go.

I arrived in the light, dropped off with nothing more than my tent, some food a pan, matches and a shovel. It wasn't a camp site, it was a spot to make a camp.

Later that night a horrific storm rolled in, I lay in my summer tent while torrential rain poured down. The wind was fierce and there was a very aggressive lightning storm and I was surrounded by trees!

No matter how tired I was or how hard I tried I just couldn't get to sleep, the storm was too violent. As the night passed into the early hours, I could feel the rivulets of water running under my tent as I lay there with my arm in the air holding the other side of the tent up off my face, the wind was so fierce it was folding my tent in two on top of me.

The wind was relentless and so was the rain. Everywhere around was so wet I had the rats running up the tent between the inner skin and the outer sheet. I wasn't sure at first if I was seeing things as I was so tired and cold having been awake all night and in and out of the tent securing tent pegs. I managed to touch this tiny little foot just to see it leap in the air and run up to the top of the tent. Now I didn't mind them being there or sheltering there, but what I did mind was that, being a summer tent it had a piece of mesh at the top of the tent as an air vent and I really didn't fancy being urinated on by rats.

About 2am; I saw my Grandmother who had passed away quite some time ago. She was a faith healer and it was I believe, her that sowed the seed of healing within me. I asked when all this torrential rain would stop and she said around 3am and it did. But she didn't tell me the wind wouldn't stop until morning. She also told me that it was time, time to start doing healing.

By 3am I was exhausted and very cold I felt to call out to the Lord and ask Him to keep me warm. Just like before I felt his presence and his warmth as He lay over my body. Within a couple of minutes I started to warm up which permitted me to stop shivering so that my muscles could relax and I could fall asleep.

In the morning, all around looked a mess, with soggy land, broken limbs of trees, it looked a mess but I was still able to light a fire to make breakfast. I was joined for breakfast by a herd of cows looking for dry land I guess or something different to eat, not to mention the array of leeches that were heading for my tent which had, incidentally remained dry all night.

That morning I had a brief glimpse of several family members who had passed. I needed that night, it was one of the most memorable nights of my life where I was shown very clearly that, not only was it time for me to start offering more healing, but also that:

"There is no death – only a change of worlds"

Looking for Children

I was driving home one evening, the roads were dry but winding. It seemed a normal evening. Half way home I saw the remnants of a car crash. There wasn't any bodies but there was a written off car, it was the only car and I could only assume the car had collided with the rocks and trees at the side of the road on the bend.

As I reached the place of the crash, I could feel the distraught energy of a woman. As I went around the bend I suddenly saw her in spirit. She was in her thirties, dark wavy hair, she was walking through the trees opposite the crash site looking for her two children. She was filled with sadness and grief. At that particular time I wasn't able to stop as I would have been a hazard to others.

However, I did send out love and compassion and I did also send out to her thoughts that she needed to go to the light and I decided that in the morning, if I felt she was still there I would pull off up the road and look for her to tell her to follow the light. My feeling was that her two children survived the crash and had been taken to hospital.

The next morning I looked for her but felt she had already gone to the light. I said some prayers for her and sent some healing to her and her children.

He Came to Say Goodbye

I was 21 years old and had been working at a nursing home but now on leave. It was 2am in the morning and I was suddenly awoken. It was Charles, Charles was a really sweet gentleman who had dementia but was happy when you took the time out to be part of his conversations. What seems like nonsense to some makes perfect sense to others. I could sense him in the room so I knew he had died.

I called work the next day to ask of him just to have my thoughts and feelings confirmed – Charles had died. I asked the nurse if she knew what time he died, she didn't but she said she would check the notes for me. I told her he died around 2am, she sounded quite baffled that I would be asking her what time he died whilst telling her he died at 2am. She came back and confirmed that his death had been recorded as 2am.

The Breeze

I was once again working in a nursing home for the elderly. I was working with a nurse at the time. It was late evening and we were turning an elderly man in his bed whilst changing his sheets. As I cradled the man in my arms so that the nurse could put the clean sheet under him, I felt something which is akin to a breeze when it touches your face.

What I felt passed straight through my body, I felt it come out of my back. The feeling was so strong that I naturally turned my head to see what it was. At that particular time, I didn't *see* anything. I only felt it. I knew what it was, I knew it was the spirit or ghost of the man I was cradling; with that in mind I said to the nurse, *"You don't need to rush he has just died."*

In complete disbelief the nurse laid the man back down to check and upon examination she was able to confirm that the man had passed quietly away. What I felt was his spirit or ghost as it left his body passing straight through mine.

Lady on the Stairs

The house was 100 years old, it was a terraced house which ironically over looked a grave yard on the eastern side. It was quite a dark house downstairs but lovely and bright on the upper level with vast views.

We hadn't been living there long when I started to think I was seeing someone out of the corner of my eye coming down the stairs at different times of the day and night. As always, it felt a little eerie even though I was so used to seeing ghosts - spirits of the deceased.

As time went on, I started to see her more. She was an older lady, quite tall and slender, she always looked some-what heavy in her demeanour as if something was weighing on her mind.

She seemed harmless enough so I permitted her to stay for a while. Then one day, I felt I needed to speak to her so I waited for her to come and asked her what happened. The feeling I had, as I don't always hear them in way of voice, was that she had fallen down the stairs and broken her neck.

And with that, she was gone. I never saw her again, it was as if she just needed to be able to tell someone that it was an accident before going to the light.

Great Grandfather Beard

I had been approached by a young woman we shall call Jean, who was concerned for her parents. There had been much disruption in her parent's home. Continual sickness, job loss, redundancies, collapse of businesses; it was all happening and the pressure and stress was taking its toll on Jean's parent's.

Her mum was now suffering with anxiety and depression and her father was suicidal. Both parents were talking about a divorce after so many years of happy marriage. But the final straw came when there was a fire in the house, fortunately no-one died but there was sufficient damage to make it un-inhabitable for the weekend whilst a big clean-up was under way.

As Jean and her parents lived so far away I offered to perform a remote house cleansing. So I would cleanse the house of negative energy and any ghosts.

Jean was more than happy for me to do this and as requested, she sent me photos of each room. This wasn't strictly necessary but it permitted me a better feel and a visual cue of the house and its energy.

I worked through each room cleansing it, praying over it and sealing it with protection. I started downstairs and worked my way upstairs, I reached about half way up the stairs when I noticed a portrait of an elderly gentleman, he looked very stern and mean. As I reached the upper rooms I could feel the presence of a stern, mean man. I knew it was the same man in the portrait. I could feel the same energy from the portrait, he was grumpy and dissatisfied with life.

I paused for a moment as I wanted to find out who this man was so I contacted Jean. What Jean told me put much into perspective. The man in the upper rooms and in the portrait on the stairs was Great Grandfather Beard. Jean went on to explain that he was apparently a mean selfish old man, his business had collapsed, he felt a failure which he took real hard and never quite recovered. He begrudged anyone else success because he felt they didn't deserve it and if anyone asked him for help, he would not give it especially if that meant they may become successful. What he himself couldn't have he didn't want anyone else to have either.

Great Grandfather Beard became so bitter that even his wife left him after many years as his bitterness was pouring out onto her; he cut everyone off and died alone as a bitter old man.

How sad! And here he was still wanting others to lose everything! Great Grandfather Beard was going to have to go.

I thanked her for the information and went back to work, the darkness upstairs felt very thick and heavy, as I made my way into the spare bedroom I walked into what felt like a blanket of black fog. It was Great Grandfather Beard, he was residing in the spare room. The energy was heavy, I lit a candle and burnt some sage.

I spent some time talking to Beard as I felt he was in need of some deep healing and after about 20 minutes I asked him to leave and follow the light. He didn't hesitate nor fight; he knew it was time to go, he had had the healing he needed to prepare him to let go and move on.

Once Beard had gone I set to work, cleansing the room and the remainder of the upstairs as he had even been in the bathroom and left his energy there. There wasn't anywhere in and around that house that he hadn't been, he really did want the family to suffer and who knows, maybe it was because nobody was there to help him when he needed it.

It took be around 3 hours to thoroughly cleanse that entire building and the outside spaces. I placed protection around the grounds and around every outside door and window.

Jean went to visit her parents that weekend and she was able to report that the house felt much lighter and happier, her parent's where starting to smile again and her mum was looking less stressed in the face. She reported that her parent's had booked a sudden holiday as they felt they needed to get away together and celebrate an up and coming anniversary. All was well, the future was looking a lot clearer and a lot more hopeful, as time went on, job offers where on the table and business started to pick up.

Not only was Great Grandfather Beard gone, but so too was his portrait.

The Ghosts of Slaves

I was on a small island in Central America, I had visited there a few times previously for a break, but this time I had come with a greater purpose.

I had been shown by Spirit / God, call it what you may that I needed to go there and perform a cleansing. There was a specific area that I needed to clean, it was an area that had been set aside many years earlier as a burial site for slaves. But it wasn't just to go and perform a cleansing and blessing of the ground and area, it was also to send the many spirits that were earthbound there to the light.

I awoke this particular morning and knew that today was the day. I was up at the crack of dawn as I didn't want other people to see or wonder what I was doing, I didn't want bystanders.

I started off in my room by burning sage and praying, praying for protection and guidance so that I would accomplish all that needed to be accomplished, then set off.

I walked off up the road whilst still burning sage and chanting prayers and blessings in my mind. Although I was specifically heading for the burial ground for the slaves, things were already starting to happen. The burial ground by the way wasn't like a burial ground, there were no markers for individual graves, it was just a plot of land that no-one wanted to buy because of all the dead people buried there.

As I walked up the dirt road, I started to see hundreds of spirits suddenly going upwards to the light. All I can compare it too is when you first open a fizzy bottle of drink and you can see hundreds of tiny bubbles coming up and disappearing, that is exactly what was happening as I cleansed, prayed and chanted, except it wasn't tiny bubbles of air going up it was deceased people. The island was having a huge cleansing.

45

Having been to this island several times previously and getting to know the locals, I was well aware that many of them tend to hang tightly onto their deceased and are often reluctant to let them go. With this in mind, it is probably quite reasonable to suppose that the deceased are also quite reluctant to leave their people behind.

I continued walking, cleansing, praying and chanting and continued to see hundreds upon hundreds of spirits/ghosts leaving to follow the light. This blessed me immensely, I felt so honoured to be such an intrinsic part of the cleansing and releasing of the island.

As I approached the burial site I could feel the distinct change in energy and although there was a deep sense of peace in the area I could feel a deep burden too, the heavy burden the slaves carried. The heaviness that only captivity can bring, whether captivity of man or beast. The heaviness of acceptance that your life is not your own and although many of these people would have been treated well, just as many wouldn't have been treated well and treating someone well does not and never will, equate to freedom. To say they should be happy as they were treated well would be pure ignorance. Fulfilling someone's basic survival needs will never replace their freedom.

I cleansed the area, and spent around 15 minutes praying and chanting on the site, and although the hot sun was now up, I was not prepared to leave until I was satisfied that the work was complete.

Once complete, I set off for home where once again, I could still see the odd spirit leaving and finally heading home.

Jack O'Lantern

It was on the very same island that I learnt of *Jack O'Lantern*, it was said that old Jack wandered the long sandy stretch of beach on the eastern side; having been seen by many locals a night. All that was seen was a moving light, a light that was said to be carried by Jack.

No-one dared venture onto this beach at night for fear of being met by Jack, this was a story that had been passed on down the generations as a warning about venturing onto that particular beach after dark.

I knew I needed to remove Jack and although there is an Irish Folklore about *Jack O'Lantern*, I am unsure as to whether that Jack was real or whether he was simply folklore.

None-the-less, this Jack was real and he needed to go to the light. Is it possible that this Jack was the original Jack O'Lantern? Who knows, I guess it is possible when you consider collective unconsciousness and think about an entire culture thinking and believing the same thing. Was it possible that the real *Jack O'Lantern* was drawn to the island by these same thoughts and beliefs? We may never know, but what I did know was that this old Jack was having a huge negative impact on the people and I had been called to do something about it.

Prior to my trip I had spent much time tuning into Jack and speaking with him letting him know that he needed to follow the light and that my intention on arriving on the island was to remove him. Although I didn't hear from him or even sense his presence, I knew on a deep level that he knew who I was and why I was going to the island.

Ironically, as soon as I arrived on the island I knew he had already gone to the light. That first evening, I looked towards the beach and could feel it was missing a presence, it was already clear. I didn't share with people about Jack and sending him to the light because I wanted to find out for myself if people had noticed he had gone.

On my next trip back to the island I started to ask about *Jack O'Lantern* asking if anyone had seen him recently. No-one had seen him, my question highlighted in many the fact that they hadn't realized until I mentioned him that actually they didn't remember seeing him for quite some time; they were now able to put him to rest with the idea that *he must have gone.*

Lady Bell

I had been called to Sedona Arizona, this was to be my second visit there, 13 years after my first visit – such a magnificent place. I had been called by Spirit to perform a cleansing on a specific rock, a rock which I had previously felt a real affinity with. A rock which I had actively been performing remote healing on; on and off during those 13 years…………

….Well - the summer solstice is well and truly over and we are now on a downward run to winter, yet, it really doesn't matter because I know I am in Sedona, Arizona and I know winters here are lovely.

The main reason I came this time was to do a clearing on Bell Rock. After spending the last 13 years working on and off with her, sending healing and holding her in ceremony I expected that the area would not be as it was 13 years ago. It wasn't. I am pleased to say that preparations had been underway prior to my arrival.

I knew whilst in England that I needed to do the clearing after the full moon, so I planned it for around the 24th June.

The full moon, or rather Super Full Moon as it was called this cycle because of its closeness to the earth and hence its extra-large appearance was this morning at 4:33am. I had awoken a 4am and knew I needed to go, this was the morning not tomorrow.

I quickly gathered what I felt I needed, medicine bag, sage oil, quartz crystal, bell rock medicine pouch and more importantly than anything else my drum. I didn't come expecting to need a drum for the clearing but that is what I was led to purchase specifically for this job, so I went with it and bought a drum.

I set off while the moon was still up shining in all her glory and dawn was only just showing signs of awakening. My trip led me past the right side of Bell Rock which was the main problematic side, as I drove past I prayed, I had already opened sacred space. I called in the four directions, calling in spirit ancestors, healers, guides and animals to be with me and work with me and through me.

Already I could see and sense things starting to happen. I parked and found the trail that led to Lady Bell as I now call her. I started praying and chanting, they knew I was coming; as I walked along I threw a spiritual net that covered the whole of Lady Bell holding all earth bound spirits in that place, not to stop them from ascending but to prevent them from running off.

As I called down healing I could see that same Rainbow Rain as I saw in the healing vision prior to coming, it was gently covering Lady Bell.

I commenced the beating of the drum, it was a single slow beat that you expect to find at a funeral march, simply, *"bung, bung, bung"*. I prayed as I spoke to the spirits that were earthbound there and told them that when the beat of the drum stops, they must go and that ancient ones were there to assist them.

Suddenly the drum stopped, and with the silence and the vibration being felt through the air, the net was lifted and spirits started to leave.

There were many tears and I could see one lady crouched down crying, her hands or rather wrists bound with rope. She had been resistant, so she had been bound up ready to be taken away.

Spirits were being ministered to, healed and assisted back to the light, it was amazing to see. I spoke to this same lady and assisted her on her way, the elders took her.

Now the drum sang another song and I chanted along with it, a chant that was given to me on my way there. That side of Lady Bell was complete. I left an offering of 3 drops of Sage, one drop for protection around that side of Lady Bell, one drop for healing and another drop as a thank-you.

I continued along the side of her which was the side that had always been more problematic. I was led to a space about half way along the side, and there she was. Lady Bell herself. She was lying with her feet at my left side, you could follow her up her legs, along her bottom which was clearly defined and you could clearly see her spine running all the way up, she curved in at the waist, widened over the ribs, she was lying on her right side facing into the rock.

As I followed her spine upwards you could see her left arm extending outwards and up along the rock side, her neck and head where on the side and her hair was fairly short.

I spent some time talking with her, you could hear that she was in pain and was feeling bruised and hurt. The majority of the spirits had been sitting on her and living off her like parasites, they were draining her of her vital energy. She was a true vortex.

She was so tired, she had been waiting for me to come; she said she had been waiting for me for so long. I offered comfort and healing which was received gratefully.

Once again, the drum began to sing, it started as it did previously with its own *"funeral march"*. Spirits were being removed, some going peacefully, some needing firm handling, some needing two guides to remove them and others needing binding and removing. The Rainbow Rain continued to fall, healing was all around.

When the time was right, the drum changed its song, back to the other song which denoted that the healing was complete on that side. All the time I was praying, talking to Spirit, talking to some of the earth bound spirits. I left the same 3 drop offering of Sage and reassured Lady Bell that I would be back.

I continued towards what I call the front of Lady Bell and then onto the far corner and repeated what I had just done, directing it to that opposite side, the side I couldn't access. I used the same prayers the same drum beats for healing.

Then things really started to happen.

I found myself speaking out with great authority, with a knowing I had not experienced before. With my drum held high in my left hand and my beater held high in my right hand whilst looking towards the sky, I found myself speaking out *"in the power invested in me"* and speaking out *"in the name of White Eagle"* (my spirit name) and found myself commanding all earth bound spirits to leave the area, as I claimed back the land.

I found myself speaking out that *"I am the Shaman for Sedona and surrounding area."* It was an unusual experience. I felt I was my true self and that what I was doing and saying really was me, maybe me from another time and place.

As before, when the time was right the drum began to sing its other song. When the time was right I moved back to the front side, and as I made my way back to the front side I was aware that I could sense some spirits hiding. I naturally started to beat another rhythm and called them out, they came without any resistance and went with guides.

As I made my way up a steep incline, heading for a specific place on Lady Bell but not knowing how I was going to get to that place, I started to drift, to topple to the left and suddenly I felt Spirit give me an almighty nudge which knocked me completely off balance and to the left which just so happened to push me where I needed to be in order to get to the place I was aiming for. (Could they not of just said, *'go to the left!!!'*)

I arrived at the part of the rock that I had been guided too and asked Spirit if it was done, it was, but I still felt to do the same on that side as I had on the other sides in order to complete the ceremony. Then and only then, I left the same 3 drop offering.

It was complete.

All names have been changed to preserve identity.

24365559R00031

Printed in Poland
by Amazon Fulfillment
Poland Sp. z o.o., Wrocław